IXL MATH WORKBOOK

T0161093

GRADE 2
ADDITION
FACTS & FLUENCY

© 2020 IXL Learning. All rights reserved. No part of this publication may be reproduced, stored in a retrieval system, or transmitted, in any form or by any means (electronic, mechanical, photocopying, recording, or otherwise) without the prior written permission of IXL Learning.

ISBN: 9781947569560
24 23 22 21 20   1 2 3 4 5

Printed in the USA

About this book

This book is designed for achieving fluency with addition facts through 10 + 10 and two-digit addition. Build your accuracy with the warm-up sections, and then increase your speed with more practice. Track your progress as you go!

WARM UP

PAGES 4–12 & 26–35

In these sections, you will work on the basics of one-digit and two-digit addition. When you are done, check your answers and write your score. Circle any problems you missed or that you found difficult. Review them.

Take as long as you need, but remember that things are about to get faster!

SPEED UP

Pages 13-25 & 36-57

Boost your speed! Time yourself with mixed addition facts up to 10 + 10 and then with two-digit addition. Write your time and score in the box.

Then keep going with the next page! Record your results in the Time & Score Log to see progress over time and set goals.

Bonus Features

Take breaks throughout the book with mazes, puzzles, and other fun activities!

Time & Score Log

Page	Time	Score
Sums to 20		
13		
14		
15		
16		
17		
20		
21		
22		
23		
24		
25		

Page	Time	Score
Two-digit addition		
36		
37		
38		
39		
40		
41		
44		
45		
46		
47		
48		
49		
52		
53		
54		
55		
56		
57		

Add.

1 + 2 = _____

8 + 2 = _____

3 + 6 = _____

5 + 3 = _____

7 + 3 = _____

1 + 3 = _____

1 + 6 = _____

3 + 10 = _____

2 + 2 = _____

2 + 3 = _____

7 + 1 = _____

6 + 2 = _____

3 + 1 = _____

2 + 5 = _____

3 + 2 = _____

1 + 8 = _____

3 + 3 = _____

1 + 4 = _____

9 + 1 = _____

10 + 2 = _____

9 + 3 = _____

3 + 8 = _____

5 + 1 = _____

4 + 2 = _____

2 + 9 = _____

2 + 1 = _____

1 + 10 = _____

1 + 1 = _____

2 + 7 = _____

3 + 4 = _____

IXL.com skill ID

YJB

For more practice, visit IXL.com or the IXL mobile app and enter this code in the search bar.

Score

_____ out of 30

Add.

4 + 5 = _____   9 + 4 = _____   2 + 4 = _____

8 + 4 = _____   6 + 4 = _____   4 + 7 = _____

1 + 4 = _____   4 + 3 = _____   4 + 6 = _____

4 + 9 = _____   4 + 4 = _____   4 + 8 = _____

3 + 4 = _____   1 + 4 = _____   4 + 10 = _____

7 + 4 = _____   4 + 2 = _____   5 + 4 = _____

6 + 4 = _____   4 + 9 = _____   8 + 4 = _____

4 + 4 = _____   4 + 5 = _____   4 + 1 = _____

3 + 4 = _____   4 + 8 = _____   7 + 4 = _____

4 + 2 = _____   10 + 4 = _____   9 + 4 = _____

IXL.com
skill ID
5T3

Score

_____ out of 30

Nice!

DATE: ___ / ___ / ___

Add.

5 + 7 = _____

5 + 4 = _____

6 + 5 = _____

3 + 5 = _____

5 + 2 = _____

1 + 5 = _____

9 + 5 = _____

5 + 1 = _____

8 + 5 = _____

5 + 5 = _____

6 + 5 = _____

5 + 9 = _____

5 + 3 = _____

10 + 5 = _____

5 + 4 = _____

8 + 5 = _____

5 + 7 = _____

5 + 10 = _____

2 + 5 = _____

5 + 6 = _____

5 + 5 = _____

5 + 1 = _____

9 + 5 = _____

7 + 5 = _____

4 + 5 = _____

5 + 5 = _____

2 + 5 = _____

5 + 8 = _____

3 + 5 = _____

5 + 10 = _____

IXL.com
skill ID
ZPK

Score

_____ out of 30

Add.

6 + 4 = _____

5 + 6 = _____

6 + 2 = _____

7 + 6 = _____

6 + 6 = _____

6 + 9 = _____

1 + 6 = _____

8 + 6 = _____

4 + 6 = _____

6 + 10 = _____

6 + 3 = _____

6 + 7 = _____

6 + 9 = _____

10 + 6 = _____

2 + 6 = _____

6 + 6 = _____

1 + 6 = _____

6 + 5 = _____

8 + 6 = _____

6 + 4 = _____

7 + 6 = _____

6 + 3 = _____

9 + 6 = _____

6 + 1 = _____

2 + 6 = _____

6 + 10 = _____

6 + 6 = _____

6 + 5 = _____

3 + 6 = _____

6 + 8 = _____

IXL.com
skill ID
RGF

Score

_____ out of 30

Well done!

DATE: ____ / ____ / ____

Add.

7 + 2 = _____

4 + 7 = _____

7 + 5 = _____

7 + 10 = _____

8 + 7 = _____

7 + 7 = _____

7 + 1 = _____

6 + 7 = _____

7 + 9 = _____

7 + 3 = _____

7 + 9 = _____

1 + 7 = _____

7 + 7 = _____

9 + 7 = _____

6 + 7 = _____

7 + 4 = _____

7 + 5 = _____

10 + 7 = _____

7 + 2 = _____

7 + 6 = _____

7 + 8 = _____

7 + 10 = _____

7 + 3 = _____

2 + 7 = _____

7 + 1 = _____

7 + 7 = _____

7 + 8 = _____

3 + 7 = _____

4 + 7 = _____

5 + 7 = _____

Add.

8 + 6 = _____   3 + 8 = _____   9 + 8 = _____

5 + 8 = _____   8 + 8 = _____   8 + 2 = _____

1 + 8 = _____   8 + 10 = _____   7 + 8 = _____

6 + 8 = _____   8 + 4 = _____   8 + 5 = _____

8 + 3 = _____   8 + 9 = _____   2 + 8 = _____

8 + 1 = _____   4 + 8 = _____   8 + 7 = _____

8 + 8 = _____   10 + 8 = _____   8 + 1 = _____

2 + 8 = _____   6 + 8 = _____   8 + 8 = _____

8 + 7 = _____   8 + 3 = _____   10 + 8 = _____

4 + 8 = _____   9 + 8 = _____   8 + 5 = _____

Score

_____ out of 30

Awesome job!

Add.

9 + 4 = _____

8 + 9 = _____

9 + 6 = _____

2 + 9 = _____

9 + 7 = _____

9 + 9 = _____

9 + 3 = _____

4 + 9 = _____

9 + 8 = _____

10 + 9 = _____

9 + 9 = _____

7 + 9 = _____

9 + 3 = _____

9 + 1 = _____

5 + 9 = _____

9 + 2 = _____

8 + 9 = _____

9 + 7 = _____

9 + 5 = _____

2 + 9 = _____

5 + 9 = _____

9 + 1 = _____

9 + 10 = _____

6 + 9 = _____

3 + 9 = _____

4 + 9 = _____

10 + 9 = _____

1 + 9 = _____

9 + 9 = _____

9 + 6 = _____

Score _____ out of 30

Keep it going!

Add.

10 + 1 = _____   10 + 9 = _____   2 + 10 = _____

10 + 10 = _____   10 + 3 = _____   8 + 10 = _____

4 + 10 = _____   7 + 10 = _____   10 + 5 = _____

10 + 8 = _____   10 + 4 = _____   6 + 10 = _____

9 + 10 = _____   10 + 10 = _____   10 + 3 = _____

10 + 5 = _____   6 + 10 = _____   1 + 10 = _____

8 + 10 = _____   2 + 10 = _____   10 + 7 = _____

1 + 10 = _____   10 + 6 = _____   10 + 10 = _____

10 + 2 = _____   9 + 10 = _____   3 + 10 = _____

5 + 10 = _____   4 + 10 = _____   7 + 10 = _____

Score

_____ out of 30

DATE: ___ / ___ / ___

Add.

$0 + 9 =$ _____

$6 + 0 =$ _____

$0 + 1 =$ _____

$8 + 0 =$ _____

$0 + 9 =$ _____

$0 + 5 =$ _____

$7 + 0 =$ _____

$0 + 0 =$ _____

$0 + 10 =$ _____

$0 + 8 =$ _____

$5 + 0 =$ _____

$4 + 0 =$ _____

$0 + 7 =$ _____

$0 + 3 =$ _____

$0 + 4 =$ _____

$10 + 0 =$ _____

$0 + 8 =$ _____

$9 + 0 =$ _____

$0 + 2 =$ _____

$5 + 0 =$ _____

$2 + 0 =$ _____

$0 + 0 =$ _____

$10 + 0 =$ _____

$0 + 6 =$ _____

$3 + 0 =$ _____

$0 + 4 =$ _____

$1 + 0 =$ _____

$7 + 0 =$ _____

$6 + 0 =$ _____

$3 + 0 =$ _____

IXL.com
skill ID
YEY

Score

_____ out of 30

Impressive!

Build up your speed! Track the time it takes to do this page.

2 + 10 = _____	3 + 8 = _____	10 + 4 = _____
7 + 10 = _____	0 + 6 = _____	1 + 10 = _____
6 + 7 = _____	4 + 8 = _____	6 + 6 = _____
5 + 9 = _____	6 + 5 = _____	4 + 4 = _____
7 + 1 = _____	6 + 9 = _____	7 + 4 = _____
8 + 5 = _____	7 + 7 = _____	9 + 8 = _____
2 + 6 = _____	5 + 2 = _____	10 + 9 = _____
10 + 8 = _____	9 + 4 = _____	8 + 6 = _____
3 + 9 = _____	7 + 8 = _____	5 + 7 = _____
9 + 9 = _____	9 + 7 = _____	3 + 4 = _____

IXL.com
skill ID
5C6

Score

_____ out of 30

Time

_____ minutes _____ seconds

Add. Don't forget to track your time!

3 + 9 = _____   6 + 6 = _____   4 + 7 = _____

10 + 1 = _____   1 + 7 = _____   9 + 8 = _____

5 + 8 = _____   8 + 4 = _____   7 + 5 = _____

9 + 9 = _____   2 + 9 = _____   9 + 7 = _____

6 + 3 = _____   10 + 3 = _____   4 + 9 = _____

7 + 6 = _____   6 + 10 = _____   9 + 0 = _____

6 + 8 = _____   5 + 4 = _____   2 + 10 = _____

9 + 6 = _____   6 + 1 = _____   3 + 3 = _____

2 + 5 = _____   9 + 5 = _____   0 + 8 = _____

8 + 7 = _____   10 + 7 = _____   5 + 10 = _____

Score

_____ out of 30

Time

_____ minutes _____ seconds

Add.

3 + 10 = _____   8 + 8 = _____   5 + 3 = _____

1 + 9 = _____   7 + 8 = _____   7 + 10 = _____

7 + 4 = _____   9 + 10 = _____   8 + 0 = _____

8 + 6 = _____   8 + 5 = _____   9 + 2 = _____

10 + 5 = _____   3 + 6 = _____   6 + 7 = _____

8 + 9 = _____   4 + 8 = _____   6 + 9 = _____

4 + 3 = _____   8 + 3 = _____   10 + 6 = _____

5 + 9 = _____   10 + 10 = _____   7 + 2 = _____

8 + 10 = _____   9 + 4 = _____   6 + 5 = _____

4 + 10 = _____   5 + 5 = _____   9 + 3 = _____

Score	Time	
_____ out of 30	_____ minutes _____ seconds	*Excellent!*

DATE: ____ / ____ / ____

Add.

9 + 4 = _____   6 + 6 = _____   4 + 4 = _____

7 + 8 = _____   1 + 5 = _____   8 + 6 = _____

2 + 10 = _____   7 + 9 = _____   4 + 3 = _____

6 + 7 = _____   8 + 8 = _____   2 + 7 = _____

8 + 4 = _____   3 + 6 = _____   9 + 10 = _____

4 + 6 = _____   10 + 7 = _____   5 + 8 = _____

7 + 7 = _____   6 + 0 = _____   9 + 5 = _____

8 + 10 = _____   3 + 9 = _____   8 + 1 = _____

7 + 5 = _____   10 + 6 = _____   3 + 10 = _____

10 + 0 = _____   6 + 9 = _____   9 + 8 = _____

IXL.com
skill ID
GLB

Score

_____ out of 30

Time

_____ minutes _____ seconds

Add.

8 + 5 = _____   10 + 2 = _____   8 + 7 = _____

10 + 5 = _____   1 + 6 = _____   9 + 3 = _____

5 + 2 = _____   3 + 3 = _____   1 + 10 = _____

4 + 5 = _____   5 + 6 = _____   4 + 8 = _____

9 + 7 = _____   10 + 4 = _____   5 + 3 = _____

8 + 9 = _____   7 + 2 = _____   9 + 6 = _____

5 + 9 = _____   2 + 6 = _____   6 + 10 = _____

9 + 1 = _____   7 + 10 = _____   5 + 5 = _____

10 + 10 = _____   4 + 9 = _____   7 + 0 = _____

6 + 3 = _____   5 + 7 = _____   6 + 8 = _____

Fantastic!

Score	Time
_____ out of 30	_____ minutes _____ seconds

DATE: / /

Add across and down to find the missing numbers.

	+	4	=	9
+		+		+
5	+		=	8
=		=		=
10	+	7	=	

4	+		=	7
+		+		+
	+	3	=	5
=		=		=
6	+	6	=	

1	+		=	5
+		+		+
	+	4	=	10
=		=		=
7	+		=	

2	+		=	9
+		+		+
	+	3	=	
=		=		=
8	+		=	

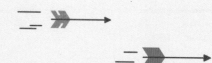

Get 20% off when you join IXL today!

Visit www.ixl.com/workbook/2fa for details.

Use the numbers to fill in the blanks. Use each number once.

2, 4, 7, 8

__2__ + __7__ = 9

__4__ + __8__ = 12

3, 5, 6, 9

_____ + _____ = 11

_____ + _____ = 12

5, 6, 8, 9

_____ + _____ = 13

_____ + _____ = 15

3, 5, 7, 8

_____ + _____ = 11

_____ + _____ = 12

3, 4, 5, 7, 8, 9

_____ + _____ = 9

_____ + _____ = 10

_____ + _____ = 17

2, 6, 7, 8, 9, 10

_____ + _____ = 12

_____ + _____ = 14

_____ + _____ = 16

Add.

$9 + 2 =$ _____ $10 + 9 =$ _____ $1 + 10 =$ _____

$0 + 9 =$ _____ $9 + 5 =$ _____ $6 + 7 =$ _____

$7 + 7 =$ _____ $8 + 3 =$ _____ $4 + 8 =$ _____

$3 + 9 =$ _____ $4 + 2 =$ _____ $7 + 10 =$ _____

$9 + 4 =$ _____ $5 + 7 =$ _____ $6 + 9 =$ _____

$7 + 4 =$ _____ $10 + 5 =$ _____ $1 + 6 =$ _____

$3 + 5 =$ _____ $5 + 6 =$ _____ $9 + 7 =$ _____

$8 + 9 =$ _____ $6 + 10 =$ _____ $4 + 5 =$ _____

$10 + 8 =$ _____ $8 + 5 =$ _____ $0 + 7 =$ _____

$6 + 6 =$ _____ $2 + 8 =$ _____ $10 + 2 =$ _____

Score _____ out of 30   Time _____ minutes _____ seconds   *Brilliant!*

Add.

10 + 6 = _____   2 + 9 = _____   5 + 1 = _____

4 + 9 = _____   8 + 10 = _____   4 + 7 = _____

2 + 4 = _____   6 + 5 = _____   8 + 4 = _____

6 + 8 = _____   9 + 3 = _____   7 + 5 = _____

5 + 9 = _____   3 + 7 = _____   8 + 8 = _____

7 + 6 = _____   5 + 8 = _____   9 + 6 = _____

3 + 10 = _____   8 + 7 = _____   0 + 10 = _____

9 + 8 = _____   5 + 10 = _____   7 + 9 = _____

6 + 2 = _____   9 + 9 = _____   10 + 10 = _____

2 + 10 = _____   1 + 8 = _____   4 + 3 = _____

IXL.com skill ID
MQX

Score

_____ out of 30

Time

_____ minutes _____ seconds

DATE: ___ / ___ / ___

Add.

5 + 6 = _____   2 + 9 = _____   1 + 6 = _____

6 + 4 = _____   8 + 5 = _____   4 + 7 = _____

7 + 8 = _____   9 + 4 = _____   3 + 3 = _____

10 + 3 = _____   8 + 8 = _____   5 + 9 = _____

6 + 7 = _____   3 + 7 = _____   2 + 10 = _____

4 + 10 = _____   1 + 10 = _____   9 + 8 = _____

9 + 0 = _____   3 + 8 = _____   8 + 6 = _____

7 + 9 = _____   9 + 9 = _____   6 + 2 = _____

9 + 6 = _____   10 + 7 = _____   4 + 8 = _____

5 + 10 = _____   1 + 5 = _____   3 + 9 = _____

IXL.com skill ID **6LC**

Score _____ out of 30

Time _____ minutes _____ seconds

Add.

7 + 10 = _____   4 + 9 = _____   5 + 7 = _____

3 + 4 = _____   6 + 6 = _____   7 + 4 = _____

7 + 6 = _____   5 + 8 = _____   5 + 2 = _____

10 + 9 = _____   7 + 7 = _____   5 + 5 = _____

6 + 8 = _____   1 + 8 = _____   6 + 9 = _____

9 + 2 = _____   9 + 7 = _____   4 + 4 = _____

7 + 0 = _____   8 + 3 = _____   10 + 2 = _____

8 + 4 = _____   9 + 5 = _____   4 + 5 = _____

10 + 1 = _____   7 + 3 = _____   8 + 7 = _____

8 + 9 = _____   10 + 6 = _____   9 + 3 = _____

Score

_____ out of 30

Time

_____ minutes _____ seconds

Nice!

Add.

2 + 9 = _____   5 + 7 = _____   6 + 10 = _____

10 + 0 = _____   10 + 5 = _____   3 + 8 = _____

7 + 7 = _____   4 + 9 = _____   2 + 6 = _____

8 + 5 = _____   10 + 8 = _____   1 + 10 = _____

7 + 10 = _____   0 + 7 = _____   10 + 9 = _____

5 + 6 = _____   8 + 8 = _____   7 + 8 = _____

4 + 3 = _____   3 + 9 = _____   8 + 6 = _____

6 + 7 = _____   9 + 6 = _____   7 + 2 = _____

8 + 9 = _____   8 + 1 = _____   4 + 7 = _____

10 + 10 = _____   7 + 9 = _____   8 + 4 = _____

Add.

4 + 8 = _____   3 + 3 = _____   5 + 9 = _____

9 + 10 = _____   2 + 5 = _____   10 + 4 = _____

7 + 4 = _____   8 + 3 = _____   6 + 9 = _____

0 + 9 = _____   9 + 8 = _____   8 + 7 = _____

9 + 7 = _____   8 + 10 = _____   4 + 2 = _____

5 + 8 = _____   9 + 9 = _____   9 + 4 = _____

10 + 7 = _____   5 + 5 = _____   7 + 5 = _____

6 + 8 = _____   3 + 10 = _____   10 + 6 = _____

8 + 2 = _____   9 + 3 = _____   1 + 7 = _____

7 + 6 = _____   3 + 6 = _____   5 + 10 = _____

Score

_____ out of 30

Time

_____ minutes _____ seconds

Incredible!

DATE: ___ / ___ / ___

Now for bigger numbers! Add.

57 + 2	22 + 5	13 + 6	34 + 4	70 + 9
62 + 6	83 + 1	40 + 8	92 + 7	33 + 4
36 + 2	15 + 4	67 + 1	91 + 8	73 + 5
46 + 1	75 + 3	60 + 9	77 + 2	23 + 4
65 + 4	42 + 6	38 + 1	14 + 4	51 + 5
94 + 2	83 + 3	35 + 3	26 + 2	54 + 4

IXL.com skill ID
EZ7

For more practice, visit IXL.com or the IXL mobile app and enter this code in the search bar.

Score

_____ out of 30

Add. Remember to regroup.

$$
\begin{array}{r} 36 \\ +7 \\ \hline \end{array}
\qquad
\begin{array}{r} 18 \\ +4 \\ \hline \end{array}
\qquad
\begin{array}{r} 72 \\ +8 \\ \hline \end{array}
\qquad
\begin{array}{r} 66 \\ +5 \\ \hline \end{array}
\qquad
\begin{array}{r} 47 \\ +4 \\ \hline \end{array}
$$

$$
\begin{array}{r} 58 \\ +5 \\ \hline \end{array}
\qquad
\begin{array}{r} 29 \\ +4 \\ \hline \end{array}
\qquad
\begin{array}{r} 84 \\ +7 \\ \hline \end{array}
\qquad
\begin{array}{r} 19 \\ +2 \\ \hline \end{array}
\qquad
\begin{array}{r} 45 \\ +5 \\ \hline \end{array}
$$

$$
\begin{array}{r} 78 \\ +6 \\ \hline \end{array}
\qquad
\begin{array}{r} 69 \\ +8 \\ \hline \end{array}
\qquad
\begin{array}{r} 25 \\ +7 \\ \hline \end{array}
\qquad
\begin{array}{r} 34 \\ +8 \\ \hline \end{array}
\qquad
\begin{array}{r} 56 \\ +9 \\ \hline \end{array}
$$

$$
\begin{array}{r} 87 \\ +9 \\ \hline \end{array}
\qquad
\begin{array}{r} 43 \\ +8 \\ \hline \end{array}
\qquad
\begin{array}{r} 52 \\ +9 \\ \hline \end{array}
\qquad
\begin{array}{r} 83 \\ +7 \\ \hline \end{array}
\qquad
\begin{array}{r} 26 \\ +6 \\ \hline \end{array}
$$

$$
\begin{array}{r} 76 \\ +4 \\ \hline \end{array}
\qquad
\begin{array}{r} 35 \\ +8 \\ \hline \end{array}
\qquad
\begin{array}{r} 39 \\ +7 \\ \hline \end{array}
\qquad
\begin{array}{r} 28 \\ +6 \\ \hline \end{array}
\qquad
\begin{array}{r} 59 \\ +5 \\ \hline \end{array}
$$

$$
\begin{array}{r} 88 \\ +7 \\ \hline \end{array}
\qquad
\begin{array}{r} 24 \\ +9 \\ \hline \end{array}
\qquad
\begin{array}{r} 67 \\ +7 \\ \hline \end{array}
\qquad
\begin{array}{r} 46 \\ +5 \\ \hline \end{array}
\qquad
\begin{array}{r} 74 \\ +8 \\ \hline \end{array}
$$

IXL.com
skill ID
8BT

Score

_____ out of 30

Great!

Add.

20 +50	30 +60	90 +10	40 +20	60 +10
10 +40	50 +30	20 +70	10 +30	70 +30
50 +50	30 +40	20 +20	70 +10	10 +10
10 +80	30 +30	60 +40	10 +20	40 +50
30 +10	50 +40	30 +50	10 +60	20 +40
80 +20	50 +10	20 +30	40 +40	20 +60

IXL.com skill ID **NPQ**

Score _____ out of 30

You've got this!

Two-digit addition

Add.

60 +24	30 +43	50 +34	20 +46	70 +18
40 +48	10 +42	40 +54	80 +16	20 +38
60 +37	70 +26	30 +51	50 +26	10 +55
40 +36	10 +38	60 +12	40 +25	20 +56
80 +13	50 +14	70 +22	30 +37	10 +72
30 +29	50 +45	20 +63	60 +28	40 +18

Score

_____ out of 30

Two-digit addition

DATE: / /

Add.

```
   5 2        2 5        1 3        3 5        2 7
 + 3 7      + 1 2      + 3 6      + 4 1      + 1 2
```

```
   1 6        2 1        4 8        2 7        2 3
 + 3 2      + 1 3      + 3 1      + 2 1      + 4 3
```

```
   3 2        1 4        5 1        1 4        4 5
 + 5 3      + 6 3      + 1 5      + 3 2      + 1 2
```

```
   4 1        7 3        6 7        7 2        2 4
 + 4 7      + 2 2      + 2 1      + 1 5      + 3 4
```

```
   3 2        4 5        3 2        1 3        5 7
 + 2 5      + 2 3      + 4 6      + 4 5      + 1 2
```

```
   8 3        2 2        3 1        6 5        2 4
 + 1 4      + 6 4      + 3 6      + 1 3      + 7 3
```

Score

_____ out of 30

Awesome job!

Two-digit addition

DATE: / /

Add.

1 8 + 2 1	6 6 + 1 2	3 8 + 1 1	2 3 + 2 4	5 5 + 1 2
4 7 + 1 2	8 4 + 1 3	2 7 + 7 1	5 8 + 4 1	1 4 + 3 3
2 4 + 3 2	3 5 + 4 4	1 5 + 4 3	3 4 + 2 3	6 3 + 2 5
7 7 + 2 1	2 1 + 3 5	3 1 + 1 8	1 3 + 4 2	4 4 + 4 2
2 6 + 4 2	6 1 + 2 4	8 5 + 1 2	2 2 + 5 4	1 7 + 6 2
5 1 + 2 7	4 2 + 5 3	3 3 + 5 3	7 2 + 1 6	5 2 + 1 4

IXL.com
skill ID
TX5

Score

_____ out of 30

Two-digit addition   DATE: / /

Add. Remember to regroup.

45 +18	24 +26	13 +38	44 +28	28 +39
16 +36	29 +56	68 +28	42 +19	24 +66
51 +39	34 +27	35 +16	78 +17	45 +35
37 +28	17 +24	53 +28	26 +66	18 +52
47 +16	14 +56	23 +38	57 +25	14 +27
72 +19	56 +36	38 +35	49 +29	68 +16

Score

_____ out of 30

Add. Remember to regroup.

48 +13	54 +38	28 +32	23 +28	18 +18
12 +29	64 +17	46 +27	76 +15	17 +33
36 +47	65 +26	25 +28	57 +28	37 +35
14 +58	23 +19	19 +48	47 +39	63 +18
26 +18	55 +27	45 +46	15 +65	39 +27
66 +19	74 +17	35 +15	77 +16	59 +16

IXL.com
skill ID
GLX

Score

_____ out of 30

Keep it going!

Add to complete each puzzle.

```
┌───┐          ┌───┐          ┌───┐
│ 4 │ +16 →   │   │ +25 →   │   │
└───┘          └───┘          └───┘
  │ +9           │ +21          │ +19
  ↓              ↓              ↓
┌───┐          ┌───┐          ┌───┐
│   │ +28 →   │   │ +23 →   │   │
└───┘          └───┘          └───┘
```

```
┌────┐          ┌───┐          ┌───┐
│ 16 │ +7 →    │   │ +49 →   │   │
└────┘          └───┘          └───┘
  │ +28          │ +40          │ +18
  ↓              ↓              ↓
┌───┐          ┌───┐          ┌───┐
│   │ +19 →   │   │ +27 →   │   │
└───┘          └───┘          └───┘
```

Boost your math learning and save 20%!
Visit www.ixl.com/workbook/2fa for details.

Time for tic-tac-toe! Find the row, column, or diagonal where all the sums are the same.

Grid 1:

24 +35 59	31 +19 50	27 +36 63
53 + 6 59	17 +42 59	46 +21 67
30 +35 65	26 +28 54	36 +23 59

(diagonal from top-left to bottom-right is marked)

Grid 2:

22 +40	67 +13	32 +43
36 +55	51 +11	54 +21
29 +41	34 +34	68 + 7

Grid 3:

43 +17	40 +31	32 +25
35 +18	27 +26	49 + 4
29 +16	45 +26	29 +25

Grid 4:

31 +27	24 +37	25 +36
43 +15	44 +17	25 +45
33 +28	35 +24	58 + 8

DATE: / /

Build up your speed! Track the time it takes you to do this page.

25 +57	32 +17	68 +16	47 +23	69 +19
17 +54	45 +35	36 +20	18 +39	46 + 7
56 +26	37 +41	73 +18	27 +29	65 +26
14 +49	38 +27	54 +36	16 +22	44 +38
33 +19	15 +58	29 +65	18 + 3	23 +45
26 +59	57 +27	29 +32	44 +43	28 +58

IXL.com skill ID GZY

Score _____ out of 30

Time _____ minutes _____ seconds

Add. Don't forget to track your time!

52 +28	27 +64	39 +47	74 +16	54 +12
57 +28	35 +18	59 +22	45 +29	27 +16
29 +36	37 + 7	13 +59	25 +35	23 +48
36 +46	14 +57	75 +13	11 +39	28 +56
60 +18	26 +26	33 +17	38 +28	16 +45
58 +24	18 +43	79 + 9	45 +23	29 +48

Nice work!

Score

_____ out of 30

Time

_____ minutes _____ seconds

DATE: / /

Add.

21 + 59	45 + 27	13 + 49	24 + 47	66 + 16
28 + 54	37 + 47	35 + 13	38 + 32	36 + 25
32 + 29	62 + 14	38 + 43	74 + 19	18 + 65
62 + 19	44 + 6	29 + 39	47 + 28	17 + 57
55 + 25	25 + 49	27 + 35	34 + 39	25 + 40
49 + 9	61 + 17	64 + 29	57 + 26	19 + 48

Score _____ out of 30

Time _____ minutes _____ seconds

Add.

5 6 + 1 4	2 6 + 3 6	3 9 + 2 1	2 5 + 4 5	8 5 + 1 3
3 5 + 4 7	4 2 + 3 5	3 9 + 2 5	3 4 + 3 7	4 2 + 1 8
2 8 + 2 6	1 6 + 3 5	2 7 + 4 7	4 4 + 2 6	3 7 + 2 5
4 9 + 1 2	6 5 + 1 9	2 2 + 4 5	3 9 + 3 9	5 3 + 8
2 8 + 4 4	2 9 + 4 3	4 7 + 2 6	6 3 + 1 7	4 8 + 4 8
3 8 + 2 0	1 5 + 7	1 9 + 3 5	5 9 + 1 8	3 4 + 2 9

Score

_____ out of 30

Time

_____ minutes _____ seconds

Fantastic!

DATE: / /

Add.

38 + 44	26 + 46	18 + 15	28 + 43	53 + 12
33 + 18	75 + 13	24 + 59	37 + 17	27 + 24
45 + 26	54 + 16	71 + 19	48 + 29	13 + 28
28 + 42	15 + 59	39 + 14	63 + 9	35 + 55
16 + 25	10 + 78	48 + 3	18 + 35	22 + 48
29 + 49	33 + 27	35 + 39	42 + 51	35 + 17

Score

_____ out of 30

Time

_____ minutes _____ seconds

Brilliant!

Add.

```
   23        38        21        15        36
 + 47      + 34      + 19      + 29      + 16


   28        35        79        12        28
 +  6      + 31      + 15      + 39      + 39


   27        48        18        18        44
 + 17      + 32      + 14      + 33      +  7


   45        29        36        72        15
 + 25      + 24      + 14      + 16      + 38


   29        37        24        35        42
 + 53      + 41      + 19      + 57      + 39


   43        17        39        44        18
 + 15      + 17      + 29      + 12      + 58
```

DATE: / /

Complete each circle. Add the two middle numbers to get the number in the outer ring.

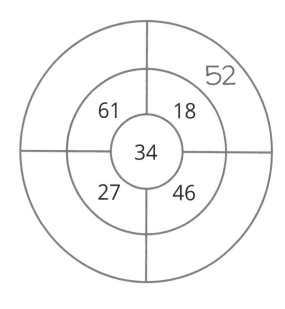

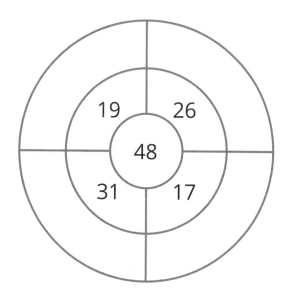

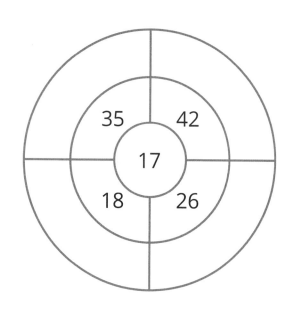

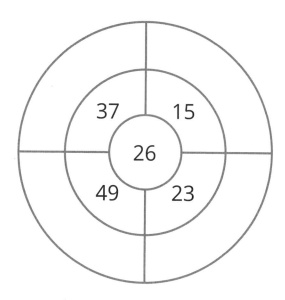

Get ahead of the curve with extra math practice!

Visit www.ixl.com/workbook/2fa for details.

Draw a path from start to finish.

If the sum is less than 40, move one square to the left.

If the sum is between 40 and 60, move one square down.

If the sum is more than 60, move one square to the right.

START ↓

35 + 1 9	26 + 1 7	20 + 1 8	24 + 6	54 + 1 6
48 + 9	22 + 3 7	33 + 1 8	36 + 1 7	44 + 2 5
38 + 2 4	50 + 1 8	37 + 2 4	63 + 8	18 + 3 8
27 + 2 2	28 + 1 1	48 + 2 6	19 + 5 7	26 + 1 6
19 + 3 3	17 + 1 8	22 + 9	24 + 2 3	15 + 1 8

FINISH ↓

DATE: / /

Add.

```
  3 1        2 6        1 9        2 3        2 5
+ 2 9      + 5 6      + 4 5      + 6 1      + 3 6
```

```
  1 6        1 2        3 7        3 5        2 9
+ 3 7      + 4 8      + 1 5      + 1 5      + 5 2
```

```
  1 6        1 5        2 7        2 8        4 7
+ 3 4      + 6 8      + 2 2      + 4 9      + 1 7
```

```
  6 1        1 7        1 8        2 7        4 8
+ 3 5      + 6 3      + 3 4      + 4 4      + 4 3
```

```
  3 4        1 8        1 4        5 7        3 9
+   8      + 3 8      + 4 9      +   5      + 4 5
```

```
  1 8        2 1        5 3        2 9        5 9
+ 2 7      + 1 4      + 2 9      + 5 9      + 1 4
```

Score

_____ out of 30

Time

_____ minutes _____ seconds

Add.

```
   4 3        5 8        2 4        3 0        2 1
 + 4 7      + 1 8      + 3 6      + 4 9      + 5 9


   2 7        2 6        2 4        2 7        3 3
 + 5 6      + 4 5      +   9      + 3 7      + 4 9


   1 9        2 7        5 3        2 9        4 8
 + 1 6      + 3 4      + 1 6      + 3 9      + 2 3


   3 9        2 9        1 6        2 7        2 4
 + 4 2      + 1 8      + 3 6      + 2 5      +   8


   5 5        2 8        1 7        4 5        3 2
 + 2 8      + 6 1      + 5 9      + 1 5      + 3 8


   5 3        1 9        2 3        3 5        6 5
 + 1 7      + 3 4      + 6 8      + 2 2      + 2 9
```

Score

_____ out of 30

Time

_____ minutes _____ seconds

Excellent!

Add.

36 + 45	25 + 62	16 + 75	47 + 24	59 + 29
46 + 16	39 + 35	51 + 29	38 + 40	13 + 77
67 + 8	18 + 19	27 + 57	45 + 38	47 + 25
56 + 14	42 + 36	54 + 26	34 + 38	57 + 4
19 + 42	23 + 39	67 + 15	49 + 35	71 + 12
14 + 18	12 + 79	48 + 28	15 + 55	12 + 68

Score _____ out of 30

Time _____ minutes _____ seconds

Nice job!

Add.

34 +39	67 +23	16 +33	28 +14	36 +25
58 +39	35 +25	18 +17	45 +18	27 + 3
34 +37	49 +29	11 +79	42 +44	29 +17
57 +17	29 +45	28 +16	58 +13	38 + 6
49 +32	76 +15	37 +13	23 +56	52 +38
62 +15	29 +33	12 +49	36 +36	25 +37

IXL.com skill ID **S5E**

Score _____ out of 30

Time _____ minutes _____ seconds

Add.

35 +19	23 +37	48 +39	25 +65	34 +22
45 +37	67 + 6	16 +31	32 +39	16 +46
58 +24	37 +27	29 +14	18 +43	14 +77
52 +29	26 +44	56 +15	19 +29	60 +17
35 +27	49 +41	13 +19	24 + 7	28 +34
18 +22	24 +51	38 +18	56 +25	15 +48

Score _____ out of 30   Time _____ minutes _____ seconds

Add.

59 + 24	47 + 33	14 + 59	16 + 26	20 + 66
18 + 37	15 + 55	54 + 18	39 + 36	29 + 31
16 + 44	37 + 34	62 + 13	46 + 25	17 + 37
42 + 49	78 + 9	59 + 33	23 + 48	45 + 19
28 + 28	15 + 27	44 + 26	18 + 5	36 + 21
53 + 23	11 + 12	43 + 37	38 + 15	59 + 19

Score

_____ out of 30

Time

_____ minutes _____ seconds

Impressive!

DATE: / /

Write the missing numbers. Each number in the pyramid is the sum of the two numbers below it.

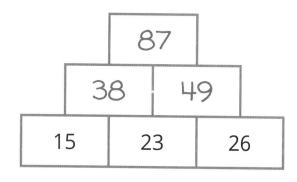

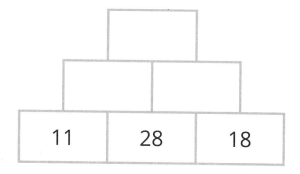

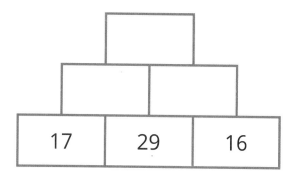

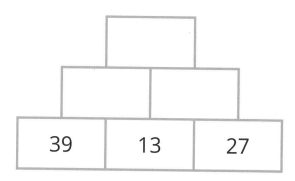

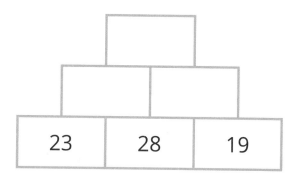

Explore hundreds more math topics!

Get 20% off when you join IXL today.

Visit www.ixl.com/workbook/2fa for details.

Complete the puzzle.

ACROSS

1. 13 + 12 = 25   **8.** 64 + 7

2. 39 + 18   **9.** 33 + 52

3. 17 + 16   **11.** 12 + 18

4. 35 + 26   **12.** 25 + 27

5. 67 + 22   **14.** 12 + 14

6. 25 + 15   **15.** 29 + 18

7. 18 + 24   **16.** 45 + 28

DOWN

1. 18 + 5   **9.** 63 + 17

2. 37 + 14   **10.** 27 + 15

3. 28 + 11   **11.** 12 + 24

4. 14 + 46   **12.** 38 + 19

5. 65 + 17   **13.** 25 + 8

7. 21 + 20

8. 57 + 18

Add.

17 + 2 3	5 4 + 7	3 9 + 1 6	1 4 + 2 5	4 6 + 3 7
3 5 + 2 7	5 4 + 3 6	4 5 + 4 5	5 7 + 3 6	3 9 + 3 1
1 5 + 3 3	4 7 + 2 7	3 8 + 1 3	1 6 + 4 3	2 7 + 1 9
2 5 + 3 6	3 2 + 4 9	2 9 + 1 9	6 8 + 2 5	2 6 + 1 1
2 4 + 2 8	2 9 + 4 3	3 1 + 2 6	4 8 + 2 2	2 3 + 9
4 9 + 3 0	5 8 + 2 8	1 5 + 5 9	3 9 + 3 4	1 6 + 4 9

Score

_____ *out of 30*

Time

_____ *minutes* _____ *seconds*

Incredible!

Add.

```
  34        32        15        24        49
+ 19      + 34      + 29      + 38      + 49


  43        15        35        32        28
+ 17      + 26      + 45      + 37      + 50


  37        59        26        18        53
+ 44      + 18      +  6      + 25      + 28


  49        18        26        46        24
+ 22      + 28      + 36      + 15      + 13


  25        11        19        28        42
+ 37      + 42      + 33      + 32      + 48


  68        14        54        28        37
+  3      + 26      + 17      + 65      + 27
```

Score

_____ out of 30

Time

_____ minutes _____ seconds

DATE: / /

Add.

25 + 29	53 + 22	43 + 17	19 + 24	27 + 57
45 + 7	39 + 59	29 + 38	18 + 13	61 + 17
12 + 44	19 + 23	38 + 12	47 + 26	51 + 39
19 + 36	26 + 45	54 + 16	64 + 8	26 + 19
59 + 12	56 + 20	35 + 47	46 + 16	27 + 24
18 + 18	17 + 25	11 + 37	54 + 45	32 + 38

IXL.com skill ID NH7

Score _____ out of 30

Time _____ minutes _____ seconds

Add.

66 +16	37 +33	12 +53	14 +29	15 +67
19 +28	67 + 5	48 +15	25 +44	39 +32
78 +19	28 +24	25 +19	43 +38	24 +32
11 +57	24 +18	49 +33	22 + 8	36 +29
37 +24	48 +27	11 +59	58 +29	52 +21
29 +27	14 +56	19 +29	36 +15	27 +37

Score

_____ out of 30

Time

_____ minutes _____ seconds

Great!

DATE: / /

Add.

36 + 24	47 + 17	59 + 11	35 + 16	17 + 66
29 + 15	12 + 55	44 + 27	28 + 38	83 + 9
49 + 42	28 + 34	25 + 13	19 + 43	18 + 34
18 + 39	16 + 72	23 + 18	76 + 16	17 + 45
15 + 25	78 + 7	42 + 26	38 + 32	16 + 21
39 + 29	47 + 13	38 + 35	14 + 19	20 + 59

Score

_____ out of 30

Time

_____ minutes _____ seconds

Add.

48 + 34	73 + 15	61 + 29	63 + 9	48 + 33
26 + 46	29 + 54	48 + 29	35 + 55	49 + 29
15 + 18	37 + 17	18 + 23	15 + 26	27 + 33
23 + 48	24 + 27	22 + 48	70 + 18	39 + 35
52 + 13	45 + 26	59 + 15	48 + 8	41 + 52
38 + 13	56 + 14	19 + 34	16 + 48	37 + 15

Score

_____ out of 30

Time

_____ minutes _____ seconds

Well done!

Answer key

PAGE 4

1 + 2 = 3	8 + 2 = 10	3 + 6 = 9
5 + 3 = 8	7 + 3 = 10	1 + 3 = 4
1 + 6 = 7	3 + 10 = 13	2 + 2 = 4
2 + 3 = 5	7 + 1 = 8	6 + 2 = 8
3 + 1 = 4	2 + 5 = 7	3 + 2 = 5
1 + 8 = 9	3 + 3 = 6	1 + 4 = 5
9 + 1 = 10	10 + 2 = 12	9 + 3 = 12
3 + 8 = 11	5 + 1 = 6	4 + 2 = 6
2 + 9 = 11	2 + 1 = 3	1 + 10 = 11
1 + 1 = 2	2 + 7 = 9	3 + 4 = 7

PAGE 5

4 + 5 = 9	9 + 4 = 13	2 + 4 = 6
8 + 4 = 12	6 + 4 = 10	4 + 7 = 11
1 + 4 = 5	4 + 3 = 7	4 + 6 = 10
4 + 9 = 13	4 + 4 = 8	4 + 8 = 12
3 + 4 = 7	1 + 4 = 5	4 + 10 = 14
7 + 4 = 11	4 + 2 = 6	5 + 4 = 9
6 + 4 = 10	4 + 9 = 13	8 + 4 = 12
4 + 4 = 8	4 + 5 = 9	4 + 1 = 5
3 + 4 = 7	4 + 8 = 12	7 + 4 = 11
4 + 2 = 6	10 + 4 = 14	9 + 4 = 13

PAGE 6

5 + 7 = 12	5 + 4 = 9	6 + 5 = 11
3 + 5 = 8	5 + 2 = 7	1 + 5 = 6
9 + 5 = 14	5 + 1 = 6	8 + 5 = 13
5 + 5 = 10	6 + 5 = 11	5 + 9 = 14
5 + 3 = 8	10 + 5 = 15	5 + 4 = 9
8 + 5 = 13	5 + 7 = 12	5 + 10 = 15
2 + 5 = 7	5 + 6 = 11	5 + 5 = 10
5 + 1 = 6	9 + 5 = 14	7 + 5 = 12
4 + 5 = 9	5 + 5 = 10	2 + 5 = 7
5 + 8 = 13	3 + 5 = 8	5 + 10 = 15

PAGE 7

6 + 4 = 10	5 + 6 = 11	6 + 2 = 8
7 + 6 = 13	6 + 6 = 12	6 + 9 = 15
1 + 6 = 7	8 + 6 = 14	4 + 6 = 10
6 + 10 = 16	6 + 3 = 9	6 + 7 = 13
6 + 9 = 15	10 + 6 = 16	2 + 6 = 8
6 + 6 = 12	1 + 6 = 7	6 + 5 = 11
8 + 6 = 14	6 + 4 = 10	7 + 6 = 13
6 + 3 = 9	9 + 6 = 15	6 + 1 = 7
2 + 6 = 8	6 + 10 = 16	6 + 6 = 12
6 + 5 = 11	3 + 6 = 9	6 + 8 = 14

PAGE 8

7 + 2 = 9	7 + 9 = 16	7 + 8 = 15
4 + 7 = 11	1 + 7 = 8	7 + 10 = 17
7 + 5 = 12	7 + 7 = 14	7 + 3 = 10
7 + 10 = 17	9 + 7 = 16	2 + 7 = 9
8 + 7 = 15	6 + 7 = 13	7 + 1 = 8
7 + 7 = 14	7 + 4 = 11	7 + 7 = 14
7 + 1 = 8	7 + 5 = 12	7 + 8 = 15
6 + 7 = 13	10 + 7 = 17	3 + 7 = 10
7 + 9 = 16	7 + 2 = 9	4 + 7 = 11
7 + 3 = 10	7 + 6 = 13	5 + 7 = 12

PAGE 9

8 + 6 = 14	3 + 8 = 11	9 + 8 = 17
5 + 8 = 13	8 + 8 = 16	8 + 2 = 10
1 + 8 = 9	8 + 10 = 18	7 + 8 = 15
6 + 8 = 14	8 + 4 = 12	8 + 5 = 13
8 + 3 = 11	8 + 9 = 17	2 + 8 = 10
8 + 1 = 9	4 + 8 = 12	8 + 7 = 15
8 + 8 = 16	10 + 8 = 18	8 + 1 = 9
2 + 8 = 10	6 + 8 = 14	8 + 8 = 16
8 + 7 = 15	8 + 3 = 11	10 + 8 = 18
4 + 8 = 12	9 + 8 = 17	8 + 5 = 13

PAGE 10

9 + 4 = 13	9 + 9 = 18	5 + 9 = 14
8 + 9 = 17	7 + 9 = 16	9 + 1 = 10
9 + 6 = 15	9 + 3 = 12	9 + 10 = 19
2 + 9 = 11	9 + 1 = 10	6 + 9 = 15
9 + 7 = 16	5 + 9 = 14	3 + 9 = 12
9 + 9 = 18	9 + 2 = 11	4 + 9 = 13
9 + 3 = 12	8 + 9 = 17	10 + 9 = 19
4 + 9 = 13	9 + 7 = 16	1 + 9 = 10
9 + 8 = 17	9 + 5 = 14	9 + 9 = 18
10 + 9 = 19	2 + 9 = 11	9 + 6 = 15

PAGE 11

10 + 1 = 11	10 + 9 = 19	2 + 10 = 12
10 + 10 = 20	10 + 3 = 13	8 + 10 = 18
4 + 10 = 14	7 + 10 = 17	10 + 5 = 15
10 + 8 = 18	10 + 4 = 14	6 + 10 = 16
9 + 10 = 19	10 + 10 = 20	10 + 3 = 13
10 + 5 = 15	6 + 10 = 16	1 + 10 = 11
8 + 10 = 18	2 + 10 = 12	10 + 7 = 17
1 + 10 = 11	10 + 6 = 16	10 + 10 = 20
10 + 2 = 12	9 + 10 = 19	3 + 10 = 13
5 + 10 = 15	4 + 10 = 14	7 + 10 = 17

PAGE 12

0 + 9 = 9	5 + 0 = 5	2 + 0 = 2
6 + 0 = 6	4 + 0 = 4	0 + 0 = 0
0 + 1 = 1	0 + 7 = 7	10 + 0 = 10
8 + 0 = 8	0 + 3 = 3	0 + 6 = 6
0 + 9 = 9	0 + 4 = 4	3 + 0 = 3
0 + 5 = 5	10 + 0 = 10	0 + 4 = 4
7 + 0 = 7	0 + 8 = 8	1 + 0 = 1
0 + 0 = 0	9 + 0 = 9	7 + 0 = 7
0 + 10 = 10	0 + 2 = 2	6 + 0 = 6
0 + 8 = 8	5 + 0 = 5	3 + 0 = 3

PAGE 13

2 + 10 = 12	3 + 8 = 11	10 + 4 = 14
7 + 10 = 17	0 + 6 = 6	1 + 10 = 11
6 + 7 = 13	4 + 8 = 12	6 + 6 = 12
5 + 9 = 14	6 + 5 = 11	4 + 4 = 8
7 + 1 = 8	6 + 9 = 15	7 + 4 = 11
8 + 5 = 13	7 + 7 = 14	9 + 8 = 17
2 + 6 = 8	5 + 2 = 7	10 + 9 = 19
10 + 8 = 18	9 + 4 = 13	8 + 6 = 14
3 + 9 = 12	7 + 8 = 15	5 + 7 = 12
9 + 9 = 18	9 + 7 = 16	3 + 4 = 7

PAGE 14

3 + 9 = 12	6 + 6 = 12	4 + 7 = 11
10 + 1 = 11	1 + 7 = 8	9 + 8 = 17
5 + 8 = 13	8 + 4 = 12	7 + 5 = 12
9 + 9 = 18	2 + 9 = 11	9 + 7 = 16
6 + 3 = 9	10 + 3 = 13	4 + 9 = 13
7 + 6 = 13	6 + 10 = 16	9 + 0 = 9
6 + 8 = 14	5 + 4 = 9	2 + 10 = 12
9 + 6 = 15	6 + 1 = 7	3 + 3 = 6
2 + 5 = 7	9 + 5 = 14	0 + 8 = 8
8 + 7 = 15	10 + 7 = 17	5 + 10 = 15

PAGE 15

3 + 10 = 13	8 + 8 = 16	5 + 3 = 8
1 + 9 = 10	7 + 8 = 15	7 + 10 = 17
7 + 4 = 11	9 + 10 = 19	8 + 0 = 8
8 + 6 = 14	8 + 5 = 13	9 + 2 = 11
10 + 5 = 15	3 + 6 = 9	6 + 7 = 13
8 + 9 = 17	4 + 8 = 12	6 + 9 = 15
4 + 3 = 7	8 + 3 = 11	10 + 6 = 16
5 + 9 = 14	10 + 10 = 20	7 + 2 = 9
8 + 10 = 18	9 + 4 = 13	6 + 5 = 11
4 + 10 = 14	5 + 5 = 10	9 + 3 = 12

PAGE 16

9 + 4 = 13	6 + 6 = 12	4 + 4 = 8
7 + 8 = 15	1 + 5 = 6	8 + 6 = 14
2 + 10 = 12	7 + 9 = 16	4 + 3 = 7
6 + 7 = 13	8 + 8 = 16	2 + 7 = 9
8 + 4 = 12	3 + 6 = 9	9 + 10 = 19
4 + 6 = 10	10 + 7 = 17	5 + 8 = 13
7 + 7 = 14	6 + 0 = 6	9 + 5 = 14
8 + 10 = 18	3 + 9 = 12	8 + 1 = 9
7 + 5 = 12	10 + 6 = 16	3 + 10 = 13
10 + 0 = 10	6 + 9 = 15	9 + 8 = 17

PAGE 17

8 + 5 = 13	10 + 2 = 12	8 + 7 = 15
10 + 5 = 15	1 + 6 = 7	9 + 3 = 12
5 + 2 = 7	3 + 3 = 6	1 + 10 = 11
4 + 5 = 9	5 + 6 = 11	4 + 8 = 12
9 + 7 = 16	10 + 4 = 14	5 + 3 = 8
8 + 9 = 17	7 + 2 = 9	9 + 6 = 15
5 + 9 = 14	2 + 6 = 8	6 + 10 = 16
9 + 1 = 10	7 + 10 = 17	5 + 5 = 10
10 + 10 = 20	4 + 9 = 13	7 + 0 = 7
6 + 3 = 9	5 + 7 = 12	6 + 8 = 14

PAGE 18

5	+	4	=	9
+		+		+
5	+	3	=	8
=		=		=
10	+	7	=	17

4	+	3	=	7
+		+		+
2	+	3	=	5
=		=		=
6	+	6	=	12

1	+	4	=	5
+		+		+
6	+	4	=	10
=		=		=
7	+	8	=	15

2	+	7	=	9
+		+		+
6	+	3	=	9
=		=		=
8	+	10	=	18

PAGE 19

Order of numbers in answers may vary.

2, 4, 7, 8

2 + 7 = 9

4 + 8 = 12

3, 5, 6, 9

5 + 6 = 11

3 + 9 = 12

5, 6, 8, 9

5 + 8 = 13

6 + 9 = 15

3, 5, 7, 8

3 + 8 = 11

5 + 7 = 12

3, 4, 5, 7, 8, 9

4 + 5 = 9

3 + 7 = 10

8 + 9 = 17

2, 6, 7, 8, 9, 10

2 + 10 = 12

6 + 8 = 14

7 + 9 = 16

PAGE 20

9 + 2 = 11	10 + 9 = 19	1 + 10 = 11
0 + 9 = 9	9 + 5 = 14	6 + 7 = 13
7 + 7 = 14	8 + 3 = 11	4 + 8 = 12
3 + 9 = 12	4 + 2 = 6	7 + 10 = 17
9 + 4 = 13	5 + 7 = 12	6 + 9 = 15
7 + 4 = 11	10 + 5 = 15	1 + 6 = 7
3 + 5 = 8	5 + 6 = 11	9 + 7 = 16
8 + 9 = 17	6 + 10 = 16	4 + 5 = 9
10 + 8 = 18	8 + 5 = 13	0 + 7 = 7
6 + 6 = 12	2 + 8 = 10	10 + 2 = 12

PAGE 21

10 + 6 = 16	2 + 9 = 11	5 + 1 = 6
4 + 9 = 13	8 + 10 = 18	4 + 7 = 11
2 + 4 = 6	6 + 5 = 11	8 + 4 = 12
6 + 8 = 14	9 + 3 = 12	7 + 5 = 12
5 + 9 = 14	3 + 7 = 10	8 + 8 = 16
7 + 6 = 13	5 + 8 = 13	9 + 6 = 15
3 + 10 = 13	8 + 7 = 15	0 + 10 = 10
9 + 8 = 17	5 + 10 = 15	7 + 9 = 16
6 + 2 = 8	9 + 9 = 18	10 + 10 = 20
2 + 10 = 12	1 + 8 = 9	4 + 3 = 7

PAGE 22

5 + 6 = 11	2 + 9 = 11	1 + 6 = 7
6 + 4 = 10	8 + 5 = 13	4 + 7 = 11
7 + 8 = 15	9 + 4 = 13	3 + 3 = 6
10 + 3 = 13	8 + 8 = 16	5 + 9 = 14
6 + 7 = 13	3 + 7 = 10	2 + 10 = 12
4 + 10 = 14	1 + 10 = 11	9 + 8 = 17
9 + 0 = 9	3 + 8 = 11	8 + 6 = 14
7 + 9 = 16	9 + 9 = 18	6 + 2 = 8
9 + 6 = 15	10 + 7 = 17	4 + 8 = 12
5 + 10 = 15	1 + 5 = 6	3 + 9 = 12

PAGE 23

7 + 10 = 17	4 + 9 = 13	5 + 7 = 12
3 + 4 = 7	6 + 6 = 12	7 + 4 = 11
7 + 6 = 13	5 + 8 = 13	5 + 2 = 7
10 + 9 = 19	7 + 7 = 14	5 + 5 = 10
6 + 8 = 14	1 + 8 = 9	6 + 9 = 15
9 + 2 = 11	9 + 7 = 16	4 + 4 = 8
7 + 0 = 7	8 + 3 = 11	10 + 2 = 12
8 + 4 = 12	9 + 5 = 14	4 + 5 = 9
10 + 1 = 11	7 + 3 = 10	8 + 7 = 15
8 + 9 = 17	10 + 6 = 16	9 + 3 = 12

PAGE 24

2 + 9 = 11	5 + 7 = 12	6 + 10 = 16
10 + 0 = 10	10 + 5 = 15	3 + 8 = 11
7 + 7 = 14	4 + 9 = 13	2 + 6 = 8
8 + 5 = 13	10 + 8 = 18	1 + 10 = 11
7 + 10 = 17	0 + 7 = 7	10 + 9 = 19
5 + 6 = 11	8 + 8 = 16	7 + 8 = 15
4 + 3 = 7	3 + 9 = 12	8 + 6 = 14
6 + 7 = 13	9 + 6 = 15	7 + 2 = 9
8 + 9 = 17	8 + 1 = 9	4 + 7 = 11
10 + 10 = 20	7 + 9 = 16	8 + 4 = 12

PAGE 25

4 + 8 = 12	3 + 3 = 6	5 + 9 = 14
9 + 10 = 19	2 + 5 = 7	10 + 4 = 14
7 + 4 = 11	8 + 3 = 11	6 + 9 = 15
0 + 9 = 9	9 + 8 = 17	8 + 7 = 15
9 + 7 = 16	8 + 10 = 18	4 + 2 = 6
5 + 8 = 13	9 + 9 = 18	9 + 4 = 13
10 + 7 = 17	5 + 5 = 10	7 + 5 = 12
6 + 8 = 14	3 + 10 = 13	10 + 6 = 16
8 + 2 = 10	9 + 3 = 12	1 + 7 = 8
7 + 6 = 13	3 + 6 = 9	5 + 10 = 15

Answer key

PAGE 26

57 + 2 = 59	22 + 5 = 27	13 + 6 = 19	34 + 4 = 38	70 + 9 = 79
62 + 6 = 68	83 + 1 = 84	40 + 8 = 48	92 + 7 = 99	33 + 4 = 37
36 + 2 = 38	15 + 4 = 19	67 + 1 = 68	91 + 8 = 99	73 + 5 = 78
46 + 1 = 47	75 + 3 = 78	60 + 9 = 69	77 + 2 = 79	23 + 4 = 27
65 + 4 = 69	42 + 6 = 48	38 + 1 = 39	14 + 4 = 18	51 + 5 = 56
94 + 2 = 96	83 + 3 = 86	35 + 3 = 38	26 + 2 = 28	54 + 4 = 58

PAGE 27

36 + 7 = 43	18 + 4 = 22	72 + 8 = 80	66 + 5 = 71	47 + 4 = 51
58 + 5 = 63	29 + 4 = 33	84 + 7 = 91	19 + 2 = 21	45 + 5 = 50
78 + 6 = 84	69 + 8 = 77	25 + 7 = 32	34 + 8 = 42	56 + 9 = 65
87 + 9 = 96	43 + 8 = 51	52 + 9 = 61	83 + 7 = 90	26 + 6 = 32
76 + 4 = 80	35 + 8 = 43	39 + 7 = 46	28 + 6 = 34	59 + 5 = 64
88 + 7 = 95	24 + 9 = 33	67 + 7 = 74	46 + 5 = 51	74 + 8 = 82

PAGE 28

20 + 50 = 70	30 + 60 = 90	90 + 10 = 100	40 + 20 = 60	60 + 10 = 70
10 + 40 = 50	50 + 30 = 80	20 + 70 = 90	10 + 30 = 40	70 + 30 = 100
50 + 50 = 100	30 + 40 = 70	20 + 20 = 40	70 + 10 = 80	10 + 10 = 20
10 + 80 = 90	30 + 30 = 60	60 + 40 = 100	10 + 20 = 30	40 + 50 = 90
30 + 10 = 40	50 + 40 = 90	30 + 50 = 80	10 + 60 = 70	20 + 40 = 60
80 + 20 = 100	50 + 10 = 60	20 + 30 = 50	40 + 40 = 80	20 + 60 = 80

PAGE 29

60 + 24 = 84	30 + 43 = 73	50 + 34 = 84	20 + 46 = 66	70 + 18 = 88
40 + 48 = 88	10 + 42 = 52	40 + 54 = 94	80 + 16 = 96	20 + 38 = 58
60 + 37 = 97	70 + 26 = 96	30 + 51 = 81	50 + 26 = 76	10 + 55 = 65
40 + 36 = 76	10 + 38 = 48	60 + 12 = 72	40 + 25 = 65	20 + 56 = 76
80 + 13 = 93	50 + 14 = 64	70 + 22 = 92	30 + 37 = 67	10 + 72 = 82
30 + 29 = 59	50 + 45 = 95	20 + 63 = 83	60 + 28 = 88	40 + 18 = 58

PAGE 30

52 + 37 = 89	25 + 12 = 37	13 + 36 = 49	35 + 41 = 76	27 + 12 = 39
16 + 32 = 48	21 + 13 = 34	48 + 31 = 79	27 + 21 = 48	23 + 43 = 66
32 + 53 = 85	14 + 63 = 77	51 + 15 = 66	14 + 32 = 46	45 + 12 = 57
41 + 47 = 88	73 + 22 = 95	67 + 21 = 88	72 + 15 = 87	24 + 34 = 58
32 + 25 = 57	45 + 23 = 68	32 + 46 = 78	13 + 45 = 58	57 + 12 = 69
83 + 14 = 97	22 + 64 = 86	31 + 36 = 67	65 + 13 = 78	24 + 73 = 97

PAGE 31

18 + 21 = 39	66 + 12 = 78	38 + 11 = 49	23 + 24 = 47	55 + 12 = 67
47 + 12 = 59	84 + 13 = 97	27 + 71 = 98	58 + 41 = 99	14 + 33 = 47
24 + 32 = 56	35 + 44 = 79	15 + 43 = 58	34 + 23 = 57	63 + 25 = 88
77 + 21 = 98	21 + 35 = 56	31 + 18 = 49	13 + 42 = 55	44 + 42 = 86
26 + 42 = 68	61 + 24 = 85	85 + 12 = 97	22 + 54 = 76	17 + 62 = 79
51 + 27 = 78	42 + 53 = 95	33 + 53 = 86	72 + 16 = 88	52 + 14 = 66

PAGE 32

45 +18 = 63	24 +26 = 50	13 +38 = 51	44 +28 = 72	28 +39 = 67
16 +36 = 52	29 +56 = 85	68 +28 = 96	42 +19 = 61	24 +66 = 90
51 +39 = 90	34 +27 = 61	35 +16 = 51	78 +17 = 95	45 +35 = 80
37 +28 = 65	17 +24 = 41	53 +28 = 81	26 +66 = 92	18 +52 = 70
47 +16 = 63	14 +56 = 70	23 +38 = 61	57 +25 = 82	14 +27 = 41
72 +19 = 91	56 +36 = 92	38 +35 = 73	49 +29 = 78	68 +16 = 84

PAGE 33

48 +13 = 61	54 +38 = 92	28 +32 = 60	23 +28 = 51	18 +18 = 36
12 +29 = 41	64 +17 = 81	46 +27 = 73	76 +15 = 91	17 +33 = 50
36 +47 = 83	65 +26 = 91	25 +28 = 53	57 +28 = 85	37 +35 = 72
14 +58 = 72	23 +19 = 42	19 +48 = 67	47 +39 = 86	63 +18 = 81
26 +18 = 44	55 +27 = 82	45 +46 = 91	15 +65 = 80	39 +27 = 66
66 +19 = 85	74 +17 = 91	35 +15 = 50	77 +16 = 93	59 +16 = 75

PAGE 34

4 → +16 → 20 → +25 → 45
+9 ↓   +21 ↓   +19 ↓
13 → +28 → 41 → +23 → 64

16 → +7 → 23 → +49 → 72
+28 ↓   +40 ↓   +18 ↓
44 → +19 → 63 → +27 → 90

PAGE 35

24 +35 = 59	31 +19 = 50	27 +36 = 63
53 + 6 = 59	17 +42 = 59	46 +21 = 67
30 +35 = 65	26 +28 = 54	36 +23 = 59
22 +40 = 62	67 +13 = 80	32 +43 = 75
36 +55 = 91	51 +11 = 62	54 +21 = 75
29 +41 = 70	34 +34 = 68	68 + 7 = 75
43 +17 = 60	40 +31 = 71	32 +25 = 57
35 +18 = 53	27 +26 = 53	49 + 4 = 53
29 +16 = 45	45 +26 = 71	29 +25 = 54
31 +27 = 58	24 +37 = 61	25 +36 = 61
43 +15 = 58	44 +17 = 61	25 +45 = 70
33 +28 = 61	35 +24 = 59	58 + 8 = 66

PAGE 36

25 +57 = 82	32 +17 = 49	68 +16 = 84	47 +23 = 70	69 +19 = 88
17 +54 = 71	45 +35 = 80	36 +20 = 56	18 +39 = 57	46 + 7 = 53
56 +26 = 82	37 +41 = 78	73 +18 = 91	27 +29 = 56	65 +26 = 91
14 +49 = 63	38 +27 = 65	54 +36 = 90	16 +22 = 38	44 +38 = 82
33 +19 = 52	15 +58 = 73	29 +65 = 94	18 + 3 = 21	23 +45 = 68
26 +59 = 85	57 +27 = 84	29 +32 = 61	44 +43 = 87	28 +58 = 86

PAGE 37

52 +28 = 80	27 +64 = 91	39 +47 = 86	74 +16 = 90	54 +12 = 66
57 +28 = 85	35 +18 = 53	59 +22 = 81	45 +29 = 74	27 +16 = 43
29 +36 = 65	37 + 7 = 44	13 +59 = 72	25 +35 = 60	23 +48 = 71
36 +46 = 82	14 +57 = 71	75 +13 = 88	11 +39 = 50	28 +56 = 84
60 +18 = 78	26 +26 = 52	33 +17 = 50	38 +28 = 66	16 +45 = 61
58 +24 = 82	18 +43 = 61	79 + 9 = 88	45 +23 = 68	29 +48 = 77

Answer key

PAGE 38

21 +59 = 80	45 +27 = 72	13 +49 = 62	24 +47 = 71	66 +16 = 82
28 +54 = 82	37 +47 = 84	35 +13 = 48	38 +32 = 70	36 +25 = 61
32 +29 = 61	62 +14 = 76	38 +43 = 81	74 +19 = 93	18 +65 = 83
62 +19 = 81	44 + 6 = 50	29 +39 = 68	47 +28 = 75	17 +57 = 74
55 +25 = 80	25 +49 = 74	27 +35 = 62	34 +39 = 73	25 +40 = 65
49 + 9 = 58	61 +17 = 78	64 +29 = 93	57 +26 = 83	19 +48 = 67

PAGE 39

56 +14 = 70	26 +36 = 62	39 +21 = 60	25 +45 = 70	85 +13 = 98
35 +47 = 82	42 +35 = 77	39 +25 = 64	34 +37 = 71	42 +18 = 60
28 +26 = 54	16 +35 = 51	27 +47 = 74	44 +26 = 70	37 +25 = 62
49 +12 = 61	65 +19 = 84	22 +45 = 67	39 +39 = 78	53 + 8 = 61
28 +44 = 72	29 +43 = 72	47 +26 = 73	63 +17 = 80	48 +48 = 96
38 +20 = 58	15 + 7 = 22	19 +35 = 54	59 +18 = 77	34 +29 = 63

PAGE 40

38 +44 = 82	26 +46 = 72	18 +15 = 33	28 +43 = 71	53 +12 = 65
33 +18 = 51	75 +13 = 88	24 +59 = 83	37 +17 = 54	27 +24 = 51
45 +26 = 71	54 +16 = 70	71 +19 = 90	48 +29 = 77	13 +28 = 41
28 +42 = 70	15 +59 = 74	39 +14 = 53	63 + 9 = 72	35 +55 = 90
16 +25 = 41	10 +78 = 88	48 + 3 = 51	18 +35 = 53	22 +48 = 70
29 +49 = 78	33 +27 = 60	35 +39 = 74	42 +51 = 93	35 +17 = 52

PAGE 41

23 +47 = 70	38 +34 = 72	21 +19 = 40	15 +29 = 44	36 +16 = 52
28 + 6 = 34	35 +31 = 66	79 +15 = 94	12 +39 = 51	28 +39 = 67
27 +17 = 44	48 +32 = 80	18 +14 = 32	18 +33 = 51	44 + 7 = 51
45 +25 = 70	29 +24 = 53	36 +14 = 50	72 +16 = 88	15 +38 = 53
29 +53 = 82	37 +41 = 78	24 +19 = 43	35 +57 = 92	42 +39 = 81
43 +15 = 58	17 +17 = 34	39 +29 = 68	44 +12 = 56	18 +58 = 76

PAGE 42

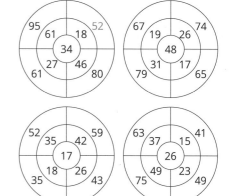

Circle 1: 95, 61, 18, 52 / 34 / 27, 46 / 61, 80
Circle 2: 67, 19, 26, 74 / 48 / 31, 17 / 79, 65
Circle 3: 52, 35, 42, 59 / 17 / 18, 26 / 35, 43
Circle 4: 63, 37, 15, 41 / 26 / 49, 23 / 75, 49

PAGE 43

START ↓

35 +19 = 54	26 +17 = 43	20 + 18 = 38	24 + 6 = 30	54 +16 = 70
48 + 9 = 57	22 +37 = 59	33 +18 = 51	36 +17 = 53	44 +25 = 69
38 +25 = 62	50 +18 = 68	37 +24 = 61	63 + 8 = 71	18 +38 = 56
27 +22 = 49	28 +11 = 39	48 +26 = 74	19 +57 = 76	26 +16 = 42
19 +33 = 52	17 +18 = 35	22 + 9 = 31	24 +23 = 47	15 +18 = 33

FINISH ↓

PAGE 44

31 +29 = 60	26 +56 = 82	19 +45 = 64	23 +61 = 84	25 +36 = 61
16 +37 = 53	12 +48 = 60	37 +15 = 52	35 +15 = 50	29 +52 = 81
16 +34 = 50	15 +68 = 83	27 +22 = 49	28 +49 = 77	47 +17 = 64
61 +35 = 96	17 +63 = 80	18 +34 = 52	27 +44 = 71	48 +43 = 91
34 + 8 = 42	18 +38 = 56	14 +49 = 63	57 + 5 = 62	39 +45 = 84
18 +27 = 45	21 +14 = 35	53 +29 = 82	29 +59 = 88	59 +14 = 73

PAGE 45

43 +47 = 90	58 +18 = 76	24 +36 = 60	30 +49 = 79	21 +59 = 80
27 +56 = 83	26 +45 = 71	24 + 9 = 33	27 +37 = 64	33 +49 = 82
19 +16 = 35	27 +34 = 61	53 +16 = 69	29 +39 = 68	48 +23 = 71
39 +42 = 81	29 +18 = 47	16 +36 = 52	27 +25 = 52	24 + 8 = 32
55 +28 = 83	28 +61 = 89	17 +59 = 76	45 +15 = 60	32 +38 = 70
53 +17 = 70	19 +34 = 53	23 +68 = 91	35 +22 = 57	65 +29 = 94

PAGE 47

34 +39 = 73	67 +23 = 90	16 +33 = 49	28 +14 = 42	36 +25 = 61
58 +39 = 97	35 +25 = 60	18 +17 = 35	45 +18 = 63	27 + 3 = 30
34 +37 = 71	49 +29 = 78	11 +79 = 90	42 +44 = 86	29 +17 = 46
57 +17 = 74	29 +45 = 74	28 +16 = 44	58 +13 = 71	38 + 6 = 44
49 +32 = 81	76 +15 = 91	37 +13 = 50	23 +56 = 79	52 +38 = 90
62 +15 = 77	29 +33 = 62	12 +49 = 61	36 +36 = 72	25 +37 = 62

PAGE 49

59 +24 = 83	47 +33 = 80	14 +59 = 73	16 +26 = 42	20 +66 = 86
18 +37 = 55	15 +55 = 70	54 +18 = 72	39 +36 = 75	29 +31 = 60
16 +44 = 60	37 +34 = 71	62 +13 = 75	46 +25 = 71	17 +37 = 54
42 +49 = 91	78 + 9 = 87	59 +33 = 92	23 +48 = 71	45 +19 = 64
28 +28 = 56	15 +27 = 42	44 +26 = 70	18 + 5 = 23	36 +21 = 57
53 +23 = 76	11 +12 = 23	43 +37 = 80	38 +15 = 53	59 +19 = 78

PAGE 46

36 +45 = 81	25 +62 = 87	16 +75 = 91	47 +24 = 71	59 +29 = 88
46 +16 = 62	39 +35 = 74	51 +29 = 80	38 +40 = 78	13 +77 = 90
67 + 8 = 75	18 +19 = 37	27 +57 = 84	45 +38 = 83	47 +25 = 72
56 +14 = 70	42 +36 = 78	54 +26 = 80	34 +38 = 72	57 + 4 = 61
19 +42 = 61	23 +39 = 62	67 +15 = 82	49 +35 = 84	71 +12 = 83
14 +18 = 32	12 +79 = 91	48 +28 = 76	15 +55 = 70	12 +68 = 80

PAGE 48

35 +19 = 54	23 +37 = 60	48 +39 = 87	25 +65 = 90	34 +22 = 56
45 +37 = 82	67 + 6 = 73	16 +31 = 47	32 +39 = 71	16 +46 = 62
58 +24 = 82	37 +27 = 64	29 +14 = 43	18 +43 = 61	14 +77 = 91
52 +29 = 81	26 +44 = 70	56 +15 = 71	19 +29 = 48	60 +17 = 77
35 +27 = 62	49 +41 = 90	13 +19 = 32	24 + 7 = 31	28 +34 = 62
18 +22 = 40	24 +51 = 75	38 +18 = 56	56 +25 = 81	15 +48 = 63

PAGE 50

Pyramid 1: 87 / 38, 49 / 15, 23, 26

Pyramid 2: 85 / 39, 46 / 11, 28, 18

Pyramid 3: 91 / 46, 45 / 17, 29, 16

Pyramid 4: 92 / 52, 40 / 39, 13, 27

Pyramid 5: 85 / 44, 41 / 19, 25, 16

Pyramid 6: 98 / 51, 47 / 23, 28, 19

PAGE 51

[1] 2	5		[2] 5	7		[3] 3	3
3		[4] 6	1		[5] 8	9	
	[6] 4	0		[7] 4	2		
			[8] 7	1			
		[9] 8	5		[10] 4		
	[11] 3	0		[12] 5	2		[13] 3
[14] 2	6		[15] 4	7		[16] 7	3

PAGE 52

17 + 23 = 40	54 + 7 = 61	39 + 16 = 55	14 + 25 = 39	46 + 37 = 83
35 + 27 = 62	54 + 36 = 90	45 + 45 = 90	57 + 36 = 93	39 + 31 = 70
15 + 33 = 48	47 + 27 = 74	38 + 13 = 51	16 + 43 = 59	27 + 19 = 46
25 + 36 = 61	32 + 49 = 81	29 + 19 = 48	68 + 25 = 93	26 + 11 = 37
24 + 28 = 52	29 + 43 = 72	31 + 26 = 57	48 + 22 = 70	23 + 9 = 32
49 + 30 = 79	58 + 28 = 86	15 + 59 = 74	39 + 34 = 73	16 + 49 = 65

PAGE 54

25 + 29 = 54	53 + 22 = 75	43 + 17 = 60	19 + 24 = 43	27 + 57 = 84
45 + 7 = 52	39 + 59 = 98	29 + 38 = 67	18 + 13 = 31	61 + 17 = 78
12 + 44 = 56	19 + 23 = 42	38 + 12 = 50	47 + 26 = 73	51 + 39 = 90
19 + 36 = 55	26 + 45 = 71	54 + 16 = 70	64 + 8 = 72	26 + 19 = 45
59 + 12 = 71	56 + 20 = 76	35 + 47 = 82	46 + 16 = 62	27 + 24 = 51
18 + 18 = 36	17 + 25 = 42	11 + 37 = 48	54 + 45 = 99	32 + 38 = 70

PAGE 56

36 + 24 = 60	47 + 17 = 64	59 + 11 = 70	35 + 16 = 51	17 + 66 = 83
29 + 15 = 44	12 + 55 = 67	44 + 27 = 71	28 + 38 = 66	83 + 9 = 92
49 + 42 = 91	28 + 34 = 62	25 + 13 = 38	19 + 43 = 62	18 + 34 = 52
18 + 39 = 57	16 + 72 = 88	23 + 18 = 41	76 + 16 = 92	17 + 45 = 62
15 + 25 = 40	78 + 7 = 85	42 + 26 = 68	38 + 32 = 70	16 + 21 = 37
39 + 29 = 68	47 + 13 = 60	38 + 35 = 73	14 + 19 = 33	20 + 59 = 79

PAGE 53

34 + 19 = 53	32 + 34 = 66	15 + 29 = 44	24 + 38 = 62	49 + 49 = 98
43 + 17 = 60	15 + 26 = 41	35 + 45 = 80	32 + 37 = 69	28 + 50 = 78
37 + 44 = 81	59 + 18 = 77	26 + 6 = 32	18 + 25 = 43	53 + 28 = 81
49 + 22 = 71	18 + 28 = 46	26 + 36 = 62	46 + 15 = 61	24 + 13 = 37
25 + 37 = 62	11 + 42 = 53	19 + 33 = 52	28 + 32 = 60	42 + 48 = 90
68 + 3 = 71	14 + 26 = 40	54 + 17 = 71	28 + 65 = 93	37 + 27 = 64

PAGE 55

66 + 16 = 82	37 + 33 = 70	12 + 53 = 65	14 + 29 = 43	15 + 67 = 82
19 + 28 = 47	67 + 5 = 72	48 + 15 = 63	25 + 44 = 69	39 + 32 = 71
78 + 19 = 97	28 + 24 = 52	25 + 19 = 44	43 + 38 = 81	24 + 32 = 56
11 + 57 = 68	24 + 18 = 42	49 + 33 = 82	22 + 8 = 30	36 + 29 = 65
37 + 24 = 61	48 + 27 = 75	11 + 59 = 70	58 + 29 = 87	52 + 21 = 73
29 + 27 = 56	14 + 56 = 70	19 + 29 = 48	36 + 15 = 51	27 + 37 = 64

PAGE 57

48 + 34 = 82	73 + 15 = 88	61 + 29 = 90	63 + 9 = 72	48 + 33 = 81
26 + 46 = 72	29 + 54 = 83	48 + 29 = 77	35 + 55 = 90	49 + 29 = 78
15 + 18 = 33	37 + 17 = 54	18 + 23 = 41	15 + 26 = 41	27 + 33 = 60
23 + 48 = 71	24 + 27 = 51	22 + 48 = 70	70 + 18 = 88	39 + 35 = 74
52 + 13 = 65	45 + 26 = 71	59 + 15 = 74	48 + 8 = 56	41 + 52 = 93
38 + 13 = 51	56 + 14 = 70	19 + 34 = 53	16 + 48 = 64	37 + 15 = 52